NO WEAKENERS

Tim Wells is made of reggae, lager top, pie and mash, and Leyton Orient FC.

No Weakeners

Published by Bad Betty Press in 2019
www.badbettypress.com

All rights reserved

The right of Tim Wells to be identified as the author of this work has been asserted by him in accordance with Section 77 of the Copyright, Designs and Patents Act of 1988.

Cover design by Amy Acre

Printed and bound in the United Kingdom

A CIP record of this book is available from the British Library.

ISBN: 978-1-913268-04-6

No Weakeners

Tim Wells

PRESS

No Weakeners

Dedicated to Jessica Samuels, S.A.G.

Contents

All the Skinhead Girls I Ever Went Out With	9
Inflammable Material	11
Each Dawn I Die	12
Boz Rock	13
Jamming So	14
Lion A De Winner	15
Wonderful World	16
Mo-Dettes	17
Looking My Love	18
Just A Feeling	19
Barbed Wire Love	20
No Pop No Style	21
Barnet Fair	22
Love Bump	23
West One (Shine On Me)	24
Ranking Slackness	25
No Bones for the Dogs	26
You I Love and Not Another	27

All the Skinhead Girls I Ever Went Out With

Were tougher
than me,
had to be.
Most could shut
a pub to silence.
All could talk
'til the Monopoly
boot came home.
The blue of
Levi jackets
and jeans
echoed
india ink
tattoos.
Their eyes
the same green
as the liquor
gracing their
double double.
On Saturday night
I heard 'Ali Baba'
and I wanted
my dream last
night last night.
Her monkey boots
scraping my shin,

the stick
of cinema carpet
as the adverts
finish
and the action begins.

Inflammable Material

The little we had was all we had.
The bands, the football, the gangs;
our own spray painted street signs.
Kung fu films saying everything
and saying it in dubbed Chinese.
Nervously asking for a pint and
hoping your sort sees you drunk,
thankful G-d made men from dirt.
Trojan tattooed on your arm,
UB40 needled right into your soul.
Shouting "I and I a conqueror" and
the girls in a line dancing 52 Girls.
Burning music shocking through;
guitars, scoring, throwing fists.
Fighting is about taking punches,
learning you knew that all along.

Each Dawn I Die

England's first World Cup
in a dozen years. Both of us
out of school and out of work.
She bowled into the boozer
drunk on summer and cider.
Lifting the sleeve of her Union
Jack tee and winking as I
clocked the Bulldog Bobby
tattoo, and my name in a
scroll. Blood seeping through
smeared Vaseline on her arm.
"You sure?" I questioned. Just
one laugh, the same sound as
a beer can opening: "We ain't
gonna get anywhere, England's
gonna lose and I want to learn
about regret."

Boz Rock

In nothing but pants, sat on the edge of the bed,
reaching back she flips the button down around herself.
Unruly breasts but it's a trimfit shirt, once buttoned
she tugs the seam and flicks her arm so the three
finger collar sits right. Red gingham check means
check yourself. The jeans are a tight squeeze, getting her
out of them was too. Boot laces are over, under, through.
When cherry red waxes lyrical it hides a multitude.
There is a haze to walk on, a wall to kick down.
The laces as tight together as we were last night.
Hand ruffles feathercut, a mouthful from a bottle
to kill the taste of morning, it's then I love her most.

Jamming So

The second time
we were together
her mum walked
into the bedroom
with a couple of
cups of char on a
tray. She was sat
on my boat. I'm
not sure what she
was doing, but it
felt pretty good.
Her mum quickly
apologised and left.
Over breakfast I
said I was very
red faced, which
didn't help. I really
needed the tea.
My mouth was dry.

Lion A De Winner

At the end
of Thundering Mantis
it truly steps forward,
they kill the old man
and the comic relief kid.
She was incensed:
"They carn't kill
the fucking kid!"
she yelled at the screen,
but they did.
After that,
Leung Kar-yan
goes beyond,
desolation follows,
reason leaves him
as he kills,
chews and eats
his adversaries.
In winning,
he loses himself.
With my arm
around her
I knew our first kiss
would be just that intense.

Wonderful World

The time I'm thinking of
Stig was outside the Robey,
tonik jacket, 501s, antiqued
boots, when the Gooners
mobbed past. Of course he
got a slap. They got him
on the floor, gave him a
shoeing. Once they were
back on their way, he got
up, shrugged his shoulders,
tugged his cravat back into
order and dusted himself
down. "Call that a kicking?"
he shouted up towards
Highbury and after 'em,
"I've had worse off me mum."

Mo-Dettes

An elbow jabbed her face. I'm not sure
it was accidental. The band were all girls,
the crowd lust. She grabbed his shirt collar,
punched once, twice, 'til he dropped.
Then danced a dance all her own.
Two kicks to the ribs then the sole
of her boot to his face. Citizen O'Brien
would've been proud. At the bar
she showed me the gap in her smile
where the tooth'd been knocked free.
"How do I look?" she asked. "I love it," I said.
Blood she spat, "Nobody's ever loved me yet."

Looking My Love

My first whistle
was a silver
grey number.
Thin lapel,
centre vent,
three button.
The bottom
never done up.
A nebbische
I am not.
White
towelling socks.
Black brogues,
white
Fred Perry.
My first whistle,
wolf that is,
was from her
as I
was bowling up
Clapton Common,
rude
and ruddy,
on a sunny
spring morning
and I
was fabulous.

Just a Feeling

Backstage
and just
the two of us left.
Everyone else
on stage,
in the band,
or giving it large
in the crowd.
We had a show
all our own.
My back
ended up carved.
She said
she'd writ
her name.
Took me
two days
to find a mirror
big enough
to peer over
me shoulder
and see.
The pain
and joy
shouted it.
She'd made a mess.
And that she excelled in.

Barbed Wire Love

At the late one on the Holloway Road
the band were on the last chorus
of The Men Behind the Wire. She rolled
the shoulders of her 'arrington, tugged
the collar of her Fred Perry, ordered a
lager top for me and Guinness for herself.
As the band started The Soldier's Song
most the bar stood up. She stayed sat
supping her pint, shamrock an' all.
"Ye're not standin'" a feller menaced.
"I stand fer no feckin' anthem," says she.
"I knows you skinheady types," he spat,
"all covered in yer Union bloody Jacks."
"Show me one on me then! There's not
one, never has been, never will be. Ye
fecker!" On her street back there in
Belfast; there was bricks, petrol bombs,
rubber bullets, and a real fight going on.

No Pop No Style

Through her teeth, she whistled.
In the alley up Cazenove Road
she lifted her skirt, pulled down
blue, white trimmed, knickers
and let it all go. Between her legs
gold, the hopes and dreams
neither of us would ever cash,
ran away into the midnight.
None too gentle, the fine spray
caught the sheen of her brogue.
She whistled 'Uptown Top Ranking'.
Through her teeth, she whistled.

Barnet Fair

Bright shined
boots gleamed,
a million girls
are born,
they do not cry
but kick.
Our Stratford's
a well trod stage.
Bleached jeans
cos magazines
can't sell us back
our grace.
Less phrenology
more Braille,
the Mars Bars
tell stories
and not a single
one sweet.
Mousy roots,
proud vermin,
white,
feathered fringe:
the cockney kids
are innocent ok.
There was Sham,
there was cider;
the Irons shirt the decider.

Love Bump

This particular evening
she sported a grey t-shirt
to pull pints in.
The 4 Skins writ large
in Lonsdale style
writing, hard pressed
to contain her glory.
A suit and an office girl
snogging in the corner.
He pestered
for a pen, "It's for
a number, it's for
a number" he pleaded.
She took a beer bottle,
smashed it, gave it him
saying "if you really
loved her,
you'd carve it on your chest."

West One (Shine on Me)

In the confines of the 100 Club,
mired in the play of passionate punk,
caught at the bar and across there's
light streaming through the peroxide
of her hair, the tilt of her head and
flash of smile. Drums staccato, a "1
– 2 – 3 – 4" the room hangs before
crashing into heat of the moment.
Sweat pours from me, my shirt sticks.
In this crush of five hundred bodies
thinking only of the press of one.
I could not move to follow her if I tried.

Ranking Slackness

Snogging
behind the bins
at school,
smell of
rubbish,
taste
of excitement.
At dusk
getting your leg
over the wall
of the
cemetery.
Her hands
firm
as she
bends double
on the
Coronation
Avenue memorial.
Abney Park
is the most
wooded
part of
the manor.

No Bones for the Dogs

Her boots shone antiqued.
Same colour as the fading
bruises on her ribs.
Her knuckles were scarred,
chopped like a rough tide
breaking on a stoic shore.
The bootlaces yellow,
pulled tight as she was.
Faded blood spotted them.
Her eyes were pea green,
plenty of honey but never
no money. Horizons
walled in by concrete.
The more she kicked the
the angrier she got. I'm not
sure if she loved fighting or
had just never known how
to be in a world without it.

You I Love and Not Another

In sleep
she balled her fists,
kept me up
with her grinding teeth.
One time
she cupped my 'nads
so tight
I had to wake her up
to let them go.
That very morning
she'd lobbed
bottles at the Chelsea.
They arced over
the traffic
on Pentonville Road.
Her love
was like that.
A hundred
sharp edges
that made a deep
and wondrous whole.
Levi jacket
sleeves folded twice.
Mars bars
on her knuckles
stood prominent.

Acknowledgements

Thanks are due to the editors of the following publications, where some of these poems previously appeared: *Welcome to Eggland, Bish Bash Bosh, Creases Like Knives, Stand Up and Spit, Rising, Anti-Hate Anthology, Street Sounds, Gob, Yeast, Hard As Nails* and *The Tally Ho*.

In June 2019 my pulp skinhead horror *Moonstomp* came out. It's a skinhead werewolf tale set in 1979. Writing it I revisited my yoof, much of which was spent at gigs and pubs, in button downs and boots, chasing, kissing, and being knocked back by girls. The women that got me through puberty were Angela Mao Ying and Ingrid Pitt. Strong women both, and most of the girls I was chasing were feathercut sorts as likely to stick the boot in as snog you.

These poems are snapshots that came as I was listening to the Ruts, Joe Gibbs, and the Mo-Dettes again and again.

Thanks for love, support, inspiration (and sometimes combination style) to the following: Adina Edwards, Salena Godden, Peyvand Sadeghian, Cheryl B, Clare Pollard, The Jones, Melisser Elliott, Booger, Julie Cheung-Inhin, Ottillie Wright, Flannery O'Connor, Becky Raw, Theresa Macauley, Aisling Rourke, Emily Harrison, Polly M Love, Sei Shonagon, Amy Cutler, and if I've missed your name you should have kissed or punched me harder.

Other titles by Bad Betty Press

Solomon's World
Jake Wild Hall

Unremember
Joel Auterson

In My Arms
Setareh Ebrahimi

The Story Is
Kate B Hall

The Dizziness Of Freedom
Edited by Amy Acre
and Jake Wild Hall

I'm Shocked
Iris Colomb

Ode to Laura Smith
Aischa Daughtery

The Pale Fox
Katie Metcalfe

TIGER
Rebecca Tamás

The Death of a Clown
Tom Bland

While I Yet Live
Gboyega Odubanjo

Raft
Anne Gill

She Too Is a Sailor
Antonia Jade King

Blank
Jake Wild Hall

And They Are Covered in Gold Light
Amy Acre

Alter Egos
Edited by Amy Acre
and Jake Wild Hall

The Body You're In
Phoebe Wagner

After the Stabbing
Xena Edwards

The Lives of the Female Poets
Clare Pollard

Give Thanks / for Shukri
Amaal Said

South of South East
Belinda Zhawi

www.ingramcontent.com/pod-product-compliance
Lightning Source LLC
Chambersburg PA
CBHW021135080526
44587CB00012B/1297